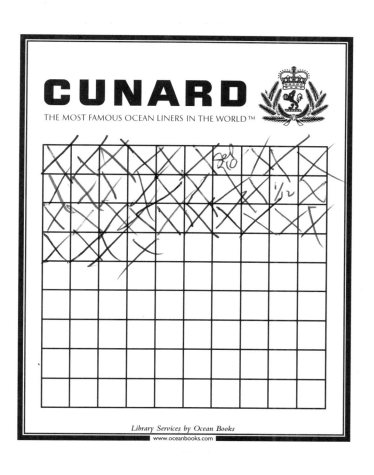

JUST LIKE THE REAL THING

Modelling Railways

JUST LIKE THE REAL THING

Modelling Railways

PETE WATERMAN

Ian Allan
PUBLISHING

JUST LIKE THE REAL THING

The inspiration for the title of this book comes from the name of the author's model company, Just Like the Real Thing. The model company prides itself in being the UK's leading modeller of 7mm rail items and also 10mm. Those who wish to find out more about Just Like the Real Thing are recommended to visit these websites

www.justliketherealthing.co.uk
www.railnuts.com

On these websites you can also view more information about Leamington Spa layout featured in this book and the modelers who work on it, as well as many of the JLRT models in action on the layout.

Acknowledgements
A big thank you to Viv Dee and Helen Dann, without whose sterling work this book couldn't have been produced. Leamington Spa is not one man's project and special credit goes to the modellers who have given up their Sundays over the last four years to realise this dream – Dave Baker, Anthony Barnes, Stuart Bracewell, Dave Byrnes, Dave Douglas, Les Fram, Geoff Holt, Brian Jones, Chris Louth, Arthur Magee, Roger Markland, Mike Raithby, Mike Taylor, Kevin Treby and the late Paul Waterman and John Dutton.

First published 2009

ISBN 978 0 7110 3455 6

Published by Ian Allan Publishing
an imprint of Ian Allan Publishing Ltd, Hersham, Surrey, KT12 4RG
Printed by Ian Allan Printing Ltd, Hersham, Surrey, KT12 4RG

Code: 0909/G2

Visit the Ian Allan website at www.ianallanpublishing.co.uk

In memory of Ron Atkinson who fostered my love for railways

CONTENTS

INTRODUCTION

After 50 years of promising myself a layout, the time was at last right for me to turn that promise into a reality.

My aim in this book is to tell the story of how we built the layout of Leamington Spa and to pass on the benefits of all the lessons we learned. In doing so I hope that you will gain knowledge from our mistakes and replicate our successes as this book takes you through the process in a step-by-step fashion. The tasks I undertook were appropriate for anyone building a railway model and therefore can be adapted to a greater or a lesser degree to suit individual requirements.

Always start with research, research and yet more research!

Photos are the most important part of any research and I was soon to learn that you can never have too many. It helped that I knew the area for our layout well and that it had been photographed many times by local photographers. I was very familiar with the work of Dick Blenkinsop as I had avidly collected all his OPC books. When I found that there was one area that I could not get enough pictures of, I called one of my oldest friends, Roger Carpenter, whose knowledge of railway photographs is second to none. He told me about another photographer, Patrick Kingston, so with Dick and Patrick's collections I started about the task.

I made over 20 visits to Leamington, taking over 1,000 pictures, and on my way home I'd always drop into Tyseley for a cup of tea with Bob Meanley. 'I've got something that might interest you,' were his words of greeting one Saturday lunchtime and out of a

big holdall came a leather bag of railway plans. They were the plans for Leamington Spa British Rail Western Region 1953, for rating purposes. What a find! This showed everything, even down to the lamp posts! It also became obvious, because it was now possible to see the full extent of the real railway layout, that we would need to make some compromises. To have built it exactly following the plans would have made the layout 230ft long and 30ft wide and, since I had no plans to buy next door's garden, we had to look at ways to compromise. Here was our first major mistake. Even though we drastically chopped the storage sidings between the Great Western and the Avenue Station, it was still far too wide to reach across - and let me tell you, sod's law dictates that if something is going to fall off, it will do so where you can't get at it! The middle of our coal sidings, therefore, really became cosmetic and because the Coventry line bears off to the right and the Birmingham line to the left on the real railway, this is what we did on our layout.

Without question, the success of this project is in no small way due to those people who built the layout and I consider myself to have been very fortunate that the majority of our modellers were guys who were, and indeed who still are, part of the Manchester Model Railway Club - a club that has always stood out for its excellence.

What makes a railway model? Now, I realise that this means different things to different people but after a lifetime of seeing other people's models and visiting such places as Pendon Museum, you start to get ideas. The first thing that became obvious to me was that I was not going to model another model layout. Personally, I think too many people have tried that and failed and it's my opinion that if you want to model a railway, then model a real one. You can chop it about and make it whatever size suits but the fact that it's a real one makes it easier in a strange way as there are rules to follow.

If not at the beginning of the work, then certainly by the end you will be multi-talented as a builder, carpenter, electrician, painter, engineer, architect and environmentalist - in other words, a dedicated Jack of All Trades! You will need to touch on areas that you'd never dreamed of before because you are about to play the Hand of God! However, the downside of this is that what the Almighty created in seven days, trust me, will take you considerably longer and it won't be as good, but you will have to take some inspiration from the way that He did it.

So many times I look at models and see that although the modeller achieved a good quality, the lack of knowledge, or, more importantly, the lack of research into the environment that the model sits in, lets the whole thing down. One group of modellers who excel in research are military modellers who make dioramas. These are quite breathtaking but we must put them into perspective since they are probably 1/32nd

BELOW: One of Wolverhampton's 'Castles' – No 7026 *Tenby Castle*, built by Paul Hannah, painted by Conrad Cooper and weathered by Fred Lewis.

scale and a big diorama is about 1ft. What we are trying to achieve is a massive diorama but with the added complication of moving parts! Even in a modest bedroom a layout of 6ft or 7ft is a big task - but not an impossible one. Our layout just needs a different approach and has to cheat the eye more than most other model layouts.

With all this knowledge on board we sat down and thought about how we would build our layout. At first it certainly was not in our minds to build Leamington Spa but we quickly realised that Leamington Spa had two things that we really needed: you can pretty well run most regions and locos through it and it stayed more or less unchanged right up to the mid 1960s so almost anything goes for visiting locos. This

BELOW: The 'Super D' waits for the signal to clear at Hatton Bank. The hopper wagons were built by Colin Foster from Parkside Dundas kits and the engine was built by Geoff Holt and presented to the author by the London & North Western Society.

latter fact might well have been why most people would have elected Leamington Spa as the ideal layout but for us there was an ever bigger rationale at play and this was that you cannot see it all in one go. The railway is on a viaduct and goes in and out of chimney pots therefore it's far more interesting to watch trains go by than it would be on just a flat board. This, coupled with seeing Dick Blenkinsop's pictures, confirmed to us that we had picked the right prototype.

Leamington Spa it was then and this is its story and like every good tale there is a moral to it – 'Build a Dream and The Dream Will Build You'!

BACKGROUND AND PRELIMINARY PLANNING

The idea for Leamington came from a group of us who regularly went to North Wales to the O Gauge Group for test run days in a local village hall and although it was a fabulous day out, the fact that we had to drive back to Warrington and Manchester meant that not a lot of drinking could be done!

It was therefore decided by four or five of us that we would like to have a track set in appropriate scenery which we could run closer to home. A few of us were members of the Manchester Model Railway Club so we had experience of that club's exhibition layouts from 2mm to 7mm. Once we had decided to build the layout, the most important thing that we did was to hold a meeting to set the rules as all of us had worked on projects that had started well but which then had ground to a halt. The upside of Leamington Spa was that it can never be taken out so therefore the timescale was as long as we wanted it to be - but that was also its downside! The pure size of it meant that it was probably a lifetime's work - or what's left of it!

LEFT: No 4215 at the head of an iron ore train passes Handford Place at the start of the viaduct. The locomotive was built by Graham Bone.

We decided to appoint Team Leaders for specific tasks and it was unanimously agreed that the Team Leader would have total overall say in that particular area. This was done for a very specific purpose in that we recognised that with any project there will always be differences of opinion. It is important in a project such as this with the longevity that it promised, to have continuity to the decision-making process and we have been very fortunate that from the beginning of the project to this time of writing, we have only lost one Team Leader and that's because he no longer models.

We agreed to work together on all aspects of the build, whether ballasting, tree making or building, but we would, at all times, be under the stewardship of the Team Leader. This proved to be an excellent plan but the discipline required to remain true to it was very challenging! It can be totally frustrating when after three hours of painstakingly working on one thing, the Team Leader says: 'No, not like that, get that up' and you have to scrap it! It is, however, the only way to work and because you are working with like-minded souls with a shared goal, it does have its lighter moments. I remember, over the course of three weekends, Antony Reeves and I were trying to build a clump of seven trees at the end of Clapham Terrace. No matter how diligent we were, we just couldn't seem to get it to look right until, that is, we caught Mike Taylor nicking them and moving them to where he wanted them! It was that sort of dogged determination that was needed on a layout such as this. Mike was Team Leader in charge of all scenery and it was his eye that was important so even though we had made what we considered to be the right tree for a particular position, if Mike wanted

BELOW: No 4061, the last 'Star' to be shedded at Wolverhampton, has just been coaled. It is built by Paul Hannah, painted by Conrad Cooper and weathered by Fred Lewis.

RIGHT: Clapham Terrace was opposite the shed at Leamington. Nowadays it is a small industrial estate but the houses have not changed other than they have tiled roofs. We have moved it slightly to the north on the layout to give us more space to work with.

RIGHT: The only thing that is not the same today at Leamington Spa station compared with when I first knew it in the 1950s is that there is no longer a GWR roundel on the front.

it for another then he took it and used it. Similarly, if anyone added anything that Mike considered inappropriate he would get the vacuum cleaner out and it would be unceremoniously sucked up that tube!

As with any labour of love, one of the key elements to its success was going to be maintaining the fun element so we decided early on that we would split Sundays into the morning when we worked on the layout and the afternoon when we would run trains. To do this we knew that once we had laid the boards we needed to put track down as fast as possible. All the track work was CAD designed by Mike Rathby who was an architect. This was then printed out to real size and stuck on the baseboards which meant that we could very quickly run since it gave us an equivalent of four round and rounds. We constantly worked to the philosophy of attacking the big things which moved the layout quickly along, then returning every now and again to have a blitz on the detail. You may think that this created a bit of a 'higgledy piggledy' picture but you'd be wrong because what it did do was avoid us getting bogged down with minutiae and thereby our interest was always maintained.

RIGHT: The curves of Hatton Bank. A Class 40 on a freight approaches on the up line.

BELOW: A busy day on Leamington Shed. No 41909 sits on Leamington Spa shed after taking coal. This engine, along with its sister No 41902, was tried on the Leamington to Rugby branch in the late 1950s.

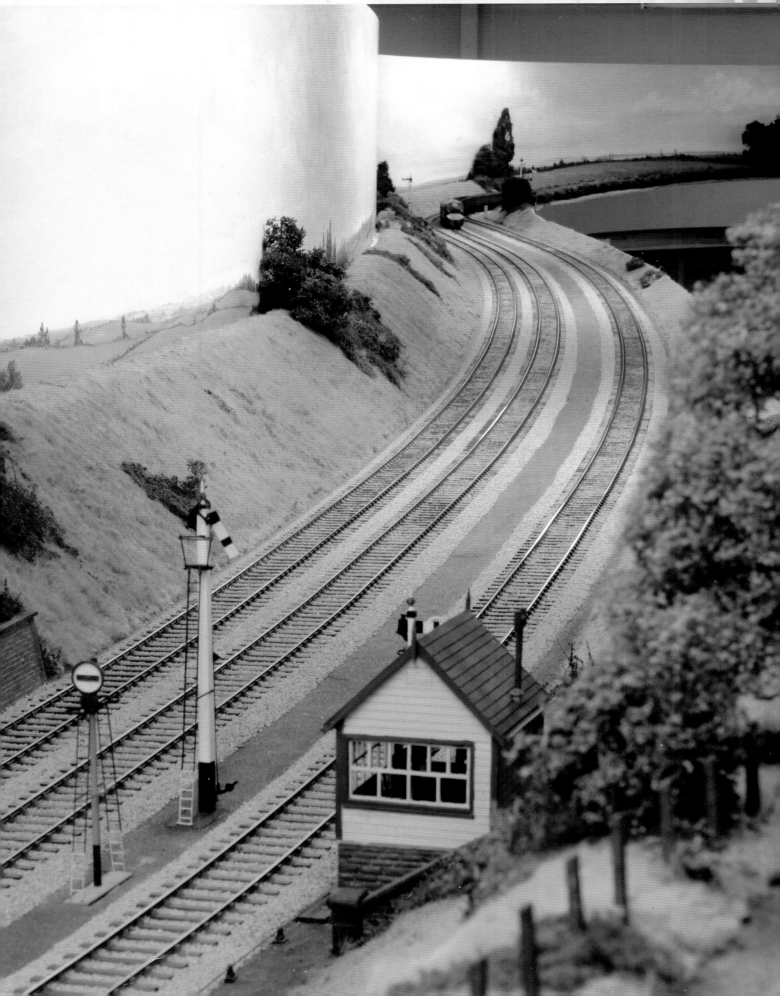

BASEBOARDS

This is the one area that we decided to have done professionally. It also helped that Dave Douglas, who is a professional carpenter, was one of our members and he, along with Mike Rathby and Mike Taylor, designed all the boards.

As you can see from the photographs, we used quite a few simple techniques. Although speed was an important element, weight also played its part. We built gradients into the layout because we definitely did not want to be part of the 'flat earth society' and Dave used laser-guided levels to do this. As already indicated in the

LEFT: No 5724 trundles through the gap between rooms.

RIGHT: The wall was knocked down to allow space between the rooms, creating the gap that can be seen in the photograph on page 21.
Dave Douglas

'Background and Preliminary' section, we glued all of the track plans onto the boards.

We were ready to start and I guess it was at this point that we realised that, just maybe, this was a big project! Our progress, driven by our enthusiasm, was swift and, because we had decided to build it in big chunks, in only eight weeks we had finished the boards and were running our first trains. Albeit on temporary track and albeit just round and round, but it was hugely significant. Having test track facilities gave us an early sense of achievement and gave us our incentive to continue.

It was at this point that we decided, because of the size of the layout, we would build it to run DCC. (I will return to DCC at a later stage.)

We had been talked into having some visitors by our friends at the North Wales Group so we decided to have an Open Day one Saturday and it turned out to attract far more interest that we had anticipated - or indeed wanted. Over 85 people turned up and because we are on a mezzanine floor on steels, we found that this amount of people, coupled with the heat they generated, created problems that took us over a year to repair. The heat caused the track to buckle and the steel floor to distort, which moved the baseboards. We discovered a simple trick was to paint a ring around the foot of the baseboard to monitor any movement. This worked very effectively and with a very simple knock it was back in place. You may find this little tip will save you a lot of time.

LEFT: The early days of the build, showing the construction of the baseboards.
Dave Douglas

RIGHT: This photograph was taken in the second room and shows the baseboards approaching the back room. *Dave Douglas*

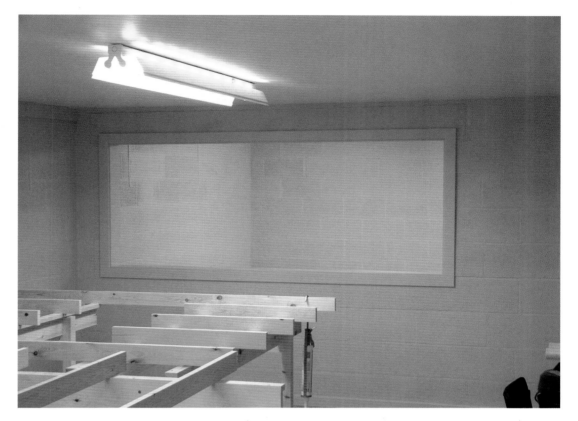

RIGHT: A view from the back room, showing the base-boards approaching the cutout. Note how wide the layout is at this point. *Dave Douglas*

LEFT: **No 46238** *City of Carlisle*, built and painted by Arthur Magee. This engine was seen regularly on the West Coast line.

BELOW: Dave Douglas's Class 28 pulls up to the signal on Hatton Bank while being passed by the author's '28'. The author's engine was built by Dave Baker and painted by Alan Brackenborough.

RIGHT: Nos 10000 and 10001 on a diversion. The engines were built and painted by Simon Atkinson.

BELOW: These tanks were regular performers in the Midlands. No 42568 was built and painted by Arthur Magee. It is seen on a local LMS service with the crimson coaches.

LEFT: A rake of Mark 1s pulled by one of Steph Torres' engines, built by Steph and lined by Conrad Cooper.

BELOW: The bottom end of Brinklow heading towards Rugby.

The blue 'King' takes a Pullman rake down the bank. This blue 'King' gets more comments than most of the other engines. You either love 'em or hate 'em, but you can't ignore them! *Tony Wright*

LAYING THE TRACK

Still using the philosophy that we needed to enjoy the layout whilst still building it, we decided to break the tracklaying tasks down into four parts:

GWR (1)
LMS (1)
GWR (2)
LMS (2)

After sticking the templates to the boards we laid the GW and LM as four loops. After a few months of enjoying the loops we started to build the track.

To build GWR 1 meant that we closed the Great Western track, which left us only the LMS to run on (and don't forget at this point it was just round a circle). Geoff Holt and Les Fram then took on the task of building all the point work, wiring and laying in the storage sidings on the Great Western side. When this was complete, the LMS was closed (LMS 1) and the Great Western opened with no points working, other than in the storage sidings. At this point, it was still a DC layout.

We then repeated the exercise on the LMS. When that was complete, we closed the Great Western again (GWR 2) and converted it to DCC (digital command control). At this stage all the point motors were fitted and made to work. When the Great Western converted to DCC it meant that we had half a layout using DCC and the other half DC.

LEFT: When building a big project to scale, everything has to be of the magnitude as seen here. This is the entry into Leamington Spa general station from the viaduct. To the right are the LMS lines. These pictures were taken before any part of the viaduct was added to the boxes.

We had always planned to allow visiting locos to run on the layout, so we decided that one loop of the LMS would be convertible to DC. The final leg was to close the LMS (LMS 2) and convert that to DCC but keep the up LMS as a convertible DC line only.

Finally, we joined the whole lot together.

Simple, eh?

Well, that might have taken only a half a page or so to explain, but it took us four years to achieve. However, despite the complexities, at no time in that four-year period were we ever unable to run trains. If people visited us or we wanted to test out anything, we could always run a train.

I expect that at this point, you may be totally impressed but I remind you that we used CAD (computer aided design) to design all this and we spent hours and hours discussing it and drawing diagrams.

It was at this point that we realised that we had cocked it all up!

Two things became absolutely blindingly obvious: (a) we didn't have enough storage space to do what we wanted to do, and, more fundamentally, (b) if a loco came from the LMS onto the GW via the Canal Loop, then we couldn't get it back onto the LMS! This problem took us over a year to resolve and culminated in a huge new junction.

The 'Waterman Underground System' was created and it is met with amazement by everyone who sees it (and occasionally with amusement). For the unsuspecting, it can be a bit of a leg pull! However, needs must and since you cannot put Great Western

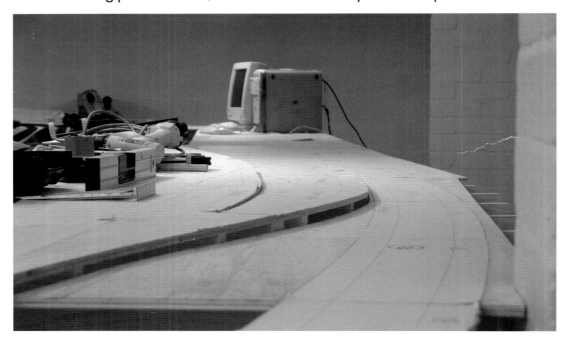

LEFT: A similar view to the picture on page 26 but from the LMS side. *Dave Douglas*

ABOVE: This view shows the same view as the previous picture but with the work nearly completed. You can now see the significance of the different levels and how the overall layout works. The picture is taken from almost the same position as opposite.

locos through LMS stations because they are out of gauge, we needed a way of putting GWR locos round Leamington without going through the Avenue Station. Hence the 'Waterman Underground System' came into being and served as a reminder that it was important to remain flexible and always be open to having to rethink ideas.

What we have just described is how to build a full layout. Or, to be more precise, what we really had at this point was a track on a baseboard, but it did mean that we were running trains. Our next task was to make it look like a railway and that's where the real work began. One of the first things we discovered was that it was better to remove the paper from the underneath a bit at a time as we laid the track and to realign it as we went along. We also discovered that we got a better result if we deviated from the CAD programme to achieve a more realistic effect. We did this only by a fraction, but by using a small mirror we found that we got a better result when viewing it with the naked eye. We pre-drilled the sleepers and used the thicker Peco track pins. All the track work on the scenic side of the layout is made with handmade C&L points and C&L track. All of the storage sidings use Peco points and Peco track.

ABOVE AND LEFT: The
different levels of
the track can clearly
be seen in these
photographs.

ABOVE: No 41909 trundles past with a perfect non-corridor suburban set. Yes, we did have some Eastern suburban sets in the Midlands!

LEFT: No 5724, built by Eric Underhill, shunts wagons in a shed area.

ABOVE: *Glastonbury Abbey* was the last 'Star' I ever saw as it was shedded at Wolverhampton. I always thought the elbow steam pipes were very attractive on these engine but then as people point out, with blue 'Kings' I have very perverse tastes!

LEFT: A 'Britannia' that I got to know only too well, No 70048 *The Territorial Army*. I must have seen this locomotive every day for months. The plate says '1908 to 1958' so the logo on the tender is obviously wrong but that's the way I like it.

RIGHT: This shows how we built the junctions on the templates and then fitted them in once they were built. With the benefit of hindsight we would have built these out of wooden sleepers.

RIGHT: Roger Manton's 'Peak' emerges from Hatton Tunnel with a rake of Mark 2 coaches.

LEFT: Going back in time once again, this shows where the signalbox was situated.

BELOW: A rake of suburban Mark 1s pulled by one of Steph Torres' engines, built by Steph and lined by Conrad Cooper.

RIGHT: A view from the opposite end of Leamington Spa station of the same general area, showing you even more complicated track work. In the foreground you can see the enormous width of the layout, which proved problematic later on.

SCENIC BOARDS

Having roughed out the whole shape of the layout from a scenic point of view with the banks, it was then time to divide the LMS from the Great Western. What I haven't mentioned before is that certain of our members don't particularly like Great Western engines so, by building a wall down the middle of the layout, we effectively created two layouts. One side of the divide was Hatton Bank and the other side was Brinklow on the West Coast main line. The great news for the LMS boys was that this was to scale and as it is also one of the fastest parts on the whole of the West Coast main line, allowing speeds of 125mph today, for all our members who put an '11' on their controllers, Brinklow was the perfect location.

This also allowed us to paint a back scene to give the impression of infinity. We were lucky in that this was started by Mike Rathby and he, along with Mike Taylor, had very strong views! Mike Rathby, being a superb artist, brought the whole layout to life. Before he started painting, we invited an electrician to come with different fluorescent tubes and light meters to check the quality of lighting as the two Mikes were very specific about the lighting that was needed. Now, this may sound very arty, and it is! It's also crucial to the success of the project because artificial lights change the colour of paint so it was important that they painted under the lighting that would give them the shades they wanted and that the entire layout was the same colour. You wouldn't believe how much trouble this caused with our older members who wanted the correct shade of LMS maroon!

LEFT: Throughout this book we have a number of pictures taken on Hatton Bank and this is what it looked like when we started to separate it from Brinklow. The track at the front is Hatton Bank and the one at the back is Brinklow. *Dave Douglas*

The lighting is still an ongoing project and as we finish each section, we move the lighting to check the area and to make sure that there are no spots brighter than others and therefore no deviation in colour.

I've seen so many backscenes that are far too vivid and therefore unrealistic. An English summer without a cloud in the sky is not something you see on a regular basis! In fact, you can guarantee that there is always more than just colour and clouds to play a major part in an English landscape. On seeing some of the pages of my previous book on my models (*A Train is For Life*, published 2008 by Ian Allan Publishing), people have suggested that we might have touched in the backscene on the photographs, but we didn't. It was all painted onto the boards, as were the trees and fields. The only thing we did avoid doing was attempt to paint a town! Once the backscene was painted, things were put in front of it to disguise it all and give it more depth and this is one of those areas where the job is never quite finished, so our backscene is an ongoing project.

BELOW: This view shows you how realistic the scenic board looks when it is finished.

RIGHT: In this photograph you can see how high the divide goes. *Dave Douglas*

RIGHT: Here we are making the tunnel at the end of Hatton, with the boards added for the scenic backdrop. *Dave Douglas*

LEFT: This shows how to make the back scenic board. Note how the tunnel is constructed.
Dave Douglas

BELOW: The back scenic board when finished. It is important not to overdo the background painting – just keep it simple.

RIGHT: This shows the back of the scenic board and the rear of the tunnel.
Dave Douglas

BELOW: Leamington's BR Standard 5 passes the scenic background.

PUTTING IN THE BANKS

The whole team was involved in researching the modeller's nightmare - that is, banks, hills, call them what you will! There are more books about how to do this than even I could afford but most of these are, in my opinion, out of date!

Today, there is a myriad of new products that are simple and very quick to use and well within most people's price range. The days of using ceiling tiles and sundealer are long gone. Most builders' merchants sell an expanded foam sheet of different thicknesses that is used in the building industry to insulate concrete. You will find that you can purchase it in sheets up to 2in thick.

Without a doubt, this is the secret ingredient contributing to the success of our layout and I cannot over emphasise my endorsement for this product, which is absolutely fantastic and will save you an unbelievable amount of time. I promise you, you will find that a sheet of this stuff will change your life! It's easy to cut, easy to use and will allow you to make your scenery in a quarter of the time of any other method. It can be sawn, heat cut, carved - but I recommend that you don't try and use a chemical solvent; trust me, it's not advisable!

The banks for us were one area that we would allow ourselves to cheat in order to enable us to do large sections at a time and, more importantly, do them very quickly. We tried lots of methods to secure the banks but in the end found that both PVA and the hot gun worked perfectly well. In fact, we found that the hot gun, which can be purchased at any DIY store, was a most useful tool for many tasks and so far we have gone through over 70 packets of glue sticks. As you can see from the photos, we

LEFT: The insulation sheet is now in place, as is the wooden wall and the tunnel entrance. You can also clearly see the track weathering.

originally used plaster to seal the joints. This was abandoned later when we realised that we could do the same using the grass (see later chapter)

The biggest thing you have to be careful of when building banks and cuttings is the steepness of the actual bank. There are two reasons for this - firstly, because on the real thing there is a limit to how steep an unsupported earth bank can be and secondly, we wanted to take pictures and so we needed to have access to the track. At the bottom of the banks there are all sorts of little bits of infrastructure that the railway puts in, such as drains, small walls, gritting trays etc, so we needed to use a little bit of imagination to get a satisfactory result. We had far more freedom on the Brinklow Banks than we did on the Hatton Bank. However, there is a limit to how much banking you can do and you have to constantly discipline your enthusiasm, remembering that you are trying to do 65ft and not 6ft!

This process, however, is always ongoing - and I guess that's the way that it will remain.

LEFT: This photograph shows how to build up the banks with insulating block. It is important to get the angle of slope correct to make sure the bank does not slip.
Dave Douglas

RIGHT: Mike Taylor starts to carve the rock cutting.

RIGHT: The rock cutting is shown with the first stone walls fitted.

LEFT: The insulation, chopped up here with a good bread knife.

ABOVE AND RIGHT: The insulation foam in its raw state and adding the plaster to the insulation foam.

THIS PAGE: The colour is then added and the grass is fitted. . . to match the real thing.

ABOVE: Sidings can be used to give you scenic breaks. As on the real railway, wagons always seem to get in the way when you want to see an engine.

LEFT: The start of the bankings and sidings at Hatton Bank.

ABOVE: Close up of
the vegetation on
the bank.

RIGHT: Stanier's 'Black 5',
No 45300, built by
Arthur Magee, plods
down Hatton.

PLATFORMS AND TUNNELS

LEFT: This is the Leamington Spa Avenue Station awning. The filigree is constructed from lasered perspex and is exactly to a standard London & North Western Railway pattern.

The platforms and tunnels on our layout were built as wooden structures that could be bolted onto the layout. Doing it this way allowed us to remove each object as one big piece so that we could more easily detail it on the bench. This meant that we avoided having to constantly reach over the model and potentially do damage to the layout, and ourselves! It also gave visitors a very quick impression of where the stations were being built. When we were completely satisfied with the platform or tunnel we then bolted it into place,

Tunnels can give some fantastic effects and they are not difficult, provided you stick to the basic rules. One of the biggest problems that I've seen is accurately modelling the banks around tunnels. What you have to think about is how steep a cutting can be and if a cutting is pretty steep you will have to add retaining walls because the railway always had to address the problem of stabilising moving earth.

Tunnels and bridges can be the modeller's best ally, and they certainly were for us. We used a tunnel to get into our fiddle sidings and we used bridges to hide the fact that the railway goes the wrong way!

All the bridges are based on those built in the area but they

RIGHT: Fitting the uprights to the roof.

are not exact copies of real bridges on the prototype. Although all four were built using standard London & North Western bridge parts their location on the layout was purely chosen by us for scenic relief.

The platforms are all made of wood and covered with paving stones. We had etched an excellent sheet of brass to do this job but we are experimenting now on some printed card. On nearly all of our station platforms we have used different styles of slabs and different surfaces but, as I have already mentioned, because they were bolted onto the layout they can all be removed, thereby giving us more freedom to change these if we wish.

BELOW: All of the woodwork is cut later but this is a typical 1890 London & North Western building and most LNWR buildings use these standard parts. You can see all of these arches at Crewe Station to this day. The Victorian builders worked in a similar way to us, using mouldings to create this grand impression.

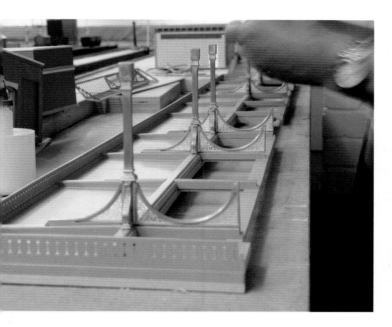

CLOCKWISE FROM ABOVE: The supports are shown from the back to the front. Fitting the canopy to the main building. The skylights are in the forefront. Fitting the canopy and skylights to the wall and platform.

LEFT: The advertising boards at the back of the station.

BELOW: What could be more appropriate than this 'Super D' pausing at the station. You will note that we have not yet fitted the station as it is slightly higher than the platform. This is to allow us to fit the other building opposite and then to align them. There is also a footbridge to be fitted.

RIGHT: The chimneys - again standard LNWR design.

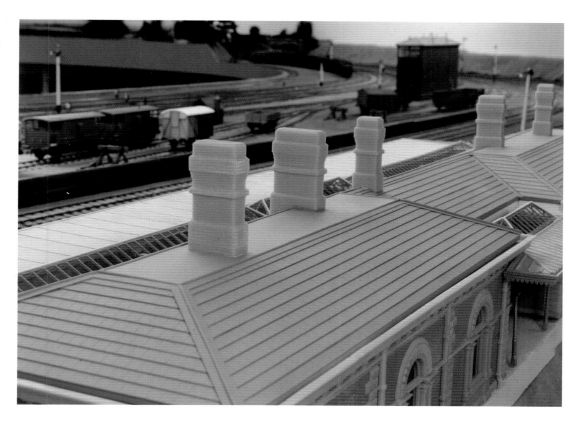

BELOW: A view from Leamington Spa General across the layout.

TRACK AND POINTS

LEFT: This is of one of Geoff Holt's junctions, plotted by Les Fram and about to be fitted. In fact, this junction is not seen at all on the layout as it is in the storage sidings.

Although we had already laid the track and points by this stage, it was time to motorise the points and look at any detailing that was to be carried out on the actual track.

Before we go any further, I just need to say that the golden rule is never to spray paint in a confined space. If you are unable to be in an open space then you must always wear a protective mask and/or have fans to extract the fumes and, if appropriate, make sure that nobody else is in the room.

One of the most important areas on a layout is the sleepers because you can see more track than anything else. The sleepers that we had decided to use for the whole of the layout were plastic but in the real world they are pine dipped in creosote. If you

RIGHT: This view is typical of most Great Western tracks, showing standard Great Western signals and the back of the repeater for the up main line. All the signals are interlocked with the track and if you look carefully you can see the junction under the bridge. The wires coming from the tunnel would pass under the track. We were amazed that nobody did these as castings.

look at railway sleepers you will see that there is a silvery brown hue to them and because we have over 2,000 yards of track, we had to come up with a method that enabled us to get this effect quickly and simply. We found a very expensive, but absolutely superb, German etched primer from the car industry which we found really bit into the plastic sleepers.

We then decided to make a track colour that we could spray in one go. By spraying the etch first and not allowing it to completely harden, and then by applying the track colour lightly, we found that the etching agent in the primer kept working and came through the track colour, giving us a silvery tinge to the finish. We then cleaned the top of the track to give it the steel shine and dry brushed rust lightly down the inside and outside of the rail only. We discovered, purely by chance that, amazingly, it seemed that the etching agent continued to work for weeks after application and after six months it gave a fantastic effect.

All the points are operated by Tortoise Point Motors, which was our preferred choice, and although we have had minor problems with them, after five years of continual use we have to report that we've had no major problems.

BELOW: Nos 10000 and 10001 double headed.

RIGHT: Pullman coaches behind *Seagull*.

BELOW: Bushes galore as No 6239 *City of Chester*, which is owned by Dave Douglas, flies by.

LEFT: The track sprayed with the primer.

BELOW: The track is then over sprayed with track dirt colour. Note how it takes on a grey sheen.

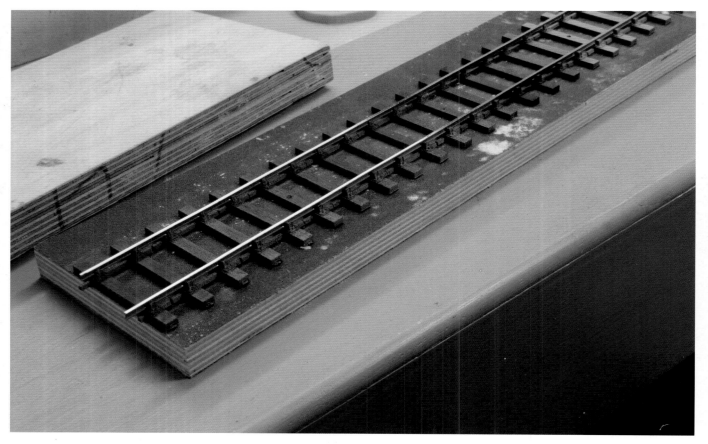

RIGHT: The top of the track is cleaned to give it a steel shine.

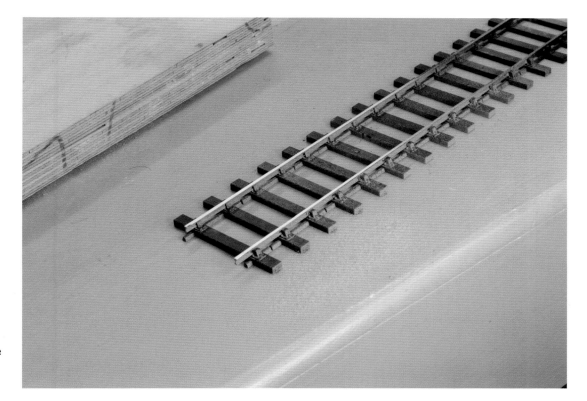

BELOW: *Seagull*. You can also see the importance of not covering the sleeper but allowing the ballast to sit to create the impression of movement.

SAND AND BALLASTING

There were two ways of looking at the sand and ballasting section of the work on the layout - it would be either the most mind numbing job that we'd ever do or, being positive, the most therapeutic job we'd ever do!

I cannot emphasise enough how difficult this task was compared with how simple the members thought it was going to be. There is more sand and ballasting on the layout than anything else and we should have known that it was never going to be simple. It would also need every member working on it and this is where the problem came. Although we needed every hand on deck, so to speak, it soon became obvious that too many cooks spoil the broth!

Although we made mistakes along the way, we soon came to the conclusion that the only sand that we could use was blast furnace sand, which had to be fine sieved. This then had to be laid and left to dry and we found that the best method was for Mike to make up the colour. I have to confess impatience set in as sometimes the process required two colourings, which did slow down the job, because there was no way that we could have approached laying the ballast until the sand had had a good two weeks to get ready. We weren't happy with playing the waiting game and still feel that this was one area which got the better of us and indeed our technique still needs some revision as the colour of the sand leached into the ballast. This is one of those things that are still in the experimental stage and where we hope that improvements can be made as time goes on.

We experimented with two sorts of ballasts, limestone and granite. We discovered that using granite is an absolute no no as the PVA sends it green and I don't care if they

LEFT: You need to have a powerful engine to get from the LMS to the Great Western lines! This is where we had to compromise because on the real railway this climb was considerably longer but this picture does show the how steep the climb is.

LEFT: The ballast in a punnet.

LEFT: Always apply the ballast with thumb and forefinger - never tip it straight out of the punnet.

use granite on the real railway as I've never seen bright green ballasts! We found that a much better effect was achieved by mixing two bags of Slaters 7mm limestone with one bag of 4mm limestone. This gave us a perfect balance but remember that when you mix it you need to get rid of the dust.

There is over 3cwt of ballast on our layout and we have discovered there is only one way to do it. The only effective method is to apply the ballast in small amounts using your thumb and forefinger then to tap it down with a small hammer - like an archaeologist. In fact, on those parts of the layout where we have deviated from the tried and tested method - maybe tried to cut a few corners - we know that at some point it will have to be taken up and redone.

When it comes to gluing the track, I've come across reams of often technical data written by many people about glue but here is my tip, and it's a simple one! Take a small plastic milk container, wash it out and fill up a third of it with PVA. Add roughly the same amount of water and then two or three squirts of washing up liquid. Mix it well (put the top on first!) and allow it to become frothy. (Please make a note on the container that this is not milk - I can testify, that it's not very pleasant if you mistake it!) Now leave the mixture to stand for at least two weeks. In this period the liquid will separate and it will give you a very good idea of how much water to how much PVA you now have. What will have also happened is that the washing up liquid will have broken the tension in the glue. After the mixture has stood for two weeks, give it another shake and you'll find that you've got a very good glue. You can now add a little more water or glue depending on what you are trying to glue and what thickness you want although I would suggest that you should keep it quite thin because it really will not move once set. Transfer some of the glue into a small bottle and apply to your track and, I promise you, it will never move.

I've seen people rubbing in alcohol at this point but God knows why! Personally, I prefer mine in pint glasses from the local brewery!

LEFT: Use a paintbrush to remove all ballast from the sleeper.

LEFT: With a small hammer tap the area around the track to lock all the stone together and make it even.

LEFT: Tap both sides.

RIGHT: Add the PVA mix.

BELOW: The finished effect.

GRASS

It was with trepidation that we approached the problem of grass because there were three big banks on the layout - Hatton Bank, Brinklow Bank and the shed area - and we knew they would be a challenge.

We had seen a small diorama where teddy bear fur had been used to make the grass and we had been so impressed with this effect that we bought a length of said fur from John at Greenscene. This was to be the most challenging thing that we'd ever done on the layout and it's fair to say that it very nearly beat us!

We must have spent over seven to eight months trying desperately to make the grass look the way that we wanted it to look and although we thought it was 'OK' we knew we could do better because Mike Taylor, our Team Leader, wasn't really jumping up and down with satisfaction at the results we'd achieved so far! We'd all got huge blisters on our hands from where we'd cut the fur down and we'd even ruined a pair of gentlemen's hair shears. Then one Sunday morning, out of pure frustration, Big Steve Naylor, not famous for his subtlety, unwittingly discovered the answer to our problems! It's funny, isn't it, how sometimes genius and downright stupidity stand side by side! Well, so it was for Steve, who happened to have a blow lamp in the boot of his car and decided, as a last resort, to set fire to the teddy bear fur! Hey, at least he had the commonsense to go outside!

I don't think even he expected such a spectacular result but, *et voila*, it worked! Because the teddy bear fur is fire retardant, it did not go up in flames but it did shrink and shrivel and with the added realism of lying in the direction that the wind had blown

LEFT: A view of Brinklow showing the various lengths of grass and gorse.

LEFT: Ron Chaplin and Pete Thompson cutting the grass and hedges.

LEFT: This shows how the bank is laid out before the final gluing.

RIGHT: Always start work on the point farthest away from you first! This shows Hatton Bank without the bank behind the signalbox.

Steve's flame, it created a fantastic realistic grass effect. This was a huge hurdle overcome because we were now able to achieve exactly the effect we wanted. By making 25ft of grass in one go we were able to cover the blue foam of the hills with green grass and create our grass banks. Now that we had solved this intimidating problem we all breathed a sigh of relief and our spirits rose as the huge expanse of grass ceased to be our nemesis and we were able to concentrate on some of the little touches that would bring the layout to life.

Today we are still working on the grass but along with static grass guns like Noka and a German Mat called Buch, we are now able to create some stunning grass effects.

LEFT: Mike and I adding the teddy bear fur in the signal area.
Dave Douglas

LEFT: Plaster added to the insulation board without the grass.
Dave Douglas

ABOVE: The LMS corner and the canal start to come together.

RIGHT: A blue foam mountain?

RIGHT: No, it's only a hill in the process of construction! Chris Louth adding trees to hide a corner.

TOP TO BOTTOM:

- Cut the fur with sharp scissors
- The teddy bear fur we use is Wolf Pattern
- Make sure you cut it right back

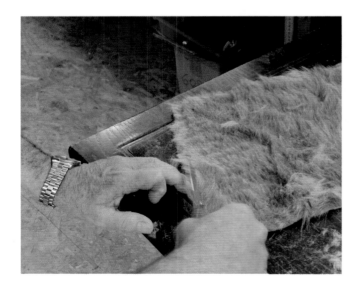

TOP TO BOTTOM:

- Use the edge of the table
- Add the poster paint with gloves
- Add to the gloves using a stick. Do not pour directly on the teddy bear fur.

LEFT: When dry, trim further using electric hair clippers.

ABOVE: Then burn the fur, keeping both the flame and the fur moving. Use the edge of the table as shown in the photograph. The fur is fire retardant and will shrivel to give you the effect of grass. Do not get too close with the flame and don't forget to keep it moving. Obviously, do not let youngsters do this.

LEFT: This is the effect you desire.

RIGHT: You can see how it looks by fitting it – it should look uneven. Remember, you can always do a bit more burning if required.

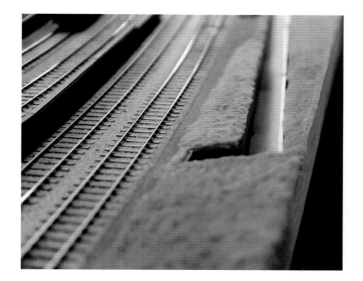

BELOW: The bits you cut off can still be used, such as here around the bottom of the signal and on the bank opposite.

TREES AND BUSHES

LEFT: If you look closely at the trees and bushes you can see that some of the bush is painted onto the back scene. The idea of this is to deceive the eye, to disguise the fact that there is another railway behind it.

The most difficult part of building the layout up to now has been creating the trees and bushes and this is where we really had to have nature lessons as well as spending lots of time taking photographs of all sorts of trees that we thought we would use. We did find that actually there was no substitute for looking at the real thing and my own garden provided lots of inspiration.

For modelling purposes, trees basically are all built in the same way - as are the bushes. We used two companies for all the tree and bush materials, Woodland Scenic and Heki, and for colours we stuck to light, medium and dark green, mixing these colours to give the impression of contrast. As mentioned elsewhere in the 'Nature' section, we selected summertime as the season to model, for the simple reason that

it's the easiest. We also made some dead trees and covered them with what was intended to be ivy.

It's far too easy to get carried away and we constantly had to remind ourselves that our layout was being built to be viewed from about 3ft away and we would have been ill advised to have overdone the scenery on just a small section because that would have looked out of context in the grand scheme of the layout and we could

RIGHT: I always spend time in the winter just to take a few snaps of the shape of trees which help when it comes to model them.

never have maintained that sort of quality throughout. We therefore had to keep hauling ourselves back from trying to overdo the minutiae of detail - this applied to every aspect of the layout and not just to trees, bushes and grass but also to the buildings and to the stock. Because we weren't building a 6ft diorama, our tasks and our goal were completely different from an exhibition layout and we had to keep reminding ourselves to tailor what we were doing to the needs of our much larger layout.

LEFT: This is the top of the bank, above Hatton Bank, showing how Mike has tapered bushes to give an impression of distance. Note also the colour of the bark.

LEFT: The end of the road seen from above. Notice the different colours in the hedge, the Great Western bracket signal in the loop and the point motor. There is still a lot of work to be done on the back bank.

THIS PAGE: This shows the only road on the layout, with a Midland Red Land Rover on it.

SIGNALS

LEFT: This is the
bracket signal with
a backboard on the
down at the start of
Hatton Bank.

The one part of the layout which was always a worry for me personally was the signalling. I don't profess to be an authority and to be honest, for me, it's probably one of the most baffling parts of railway operations. Because of the amount of photographs that we had accumulated before we started the programme, we were pretty confident that we had got pictures of every signal that we would be modelling. However, because we had made some adjustments for size reasons on the track layout, the signalling in some of the photos was inapplicable and although the South signal box was perfect, the North box, because of the way that the real signal box was sighted, did not quite work, and it will have to be replaced.

We were lucky that in life there is always someone who finds interest in the most unusual things and a chance meeting with Roger Markand (via Dave Baker) introduced us to probably the only man I know who could get excited about the pure scale of the signals! There were over 50 to be made and not just made, but made to work!

This is where Dave Burns and Arthur Magee came in. Arthur had come up with a very simple method using memory wire - and we found that the Belgium memory wire was the best. As Roger built them it was Arthur and Dave's jobs to make them work and when we fitted these fully operational signals to the layout we found that it gave a 3D effect and the whole thing took on a completely different appearance.

ABOVE LEFT TO RIGHT: The typical GWR short arm signals at the end of the up platform; the signal at the entry to the station; the signal at the end of the viaduct.

LEFT: No 4215 passes signals with a train of coal hopper wagons

RIGHT: A 70ft distance signal. This is purely fictional but we like it. You will note that the background on the lower arm is black not white because the signal is yellow and needs to stand out.

A view showing the entrance/exit signals to the station.

BUILDINGS

Generally, the Achilles' heel of most people's layouts is buildings, perhaps because they are a lot more prevalent than people originally think them to be. Because of the task we set ourselves with the Leamington Spa layout, we had to approach the modelling of buildings from a completely different perspective to that of the other elements of the layout.

Right from the beginning we were faced with a couple of options: we could have just used the available pre-printed card buildings, but this was quickly decided against since they were not prototypical and really did not represent the buildings we were modelling, or we had the option to make the buildings from foam board covered in plaster card and to make plastic kits. Our decision was to use a mixture of both plaster card and plastic kits as this was considered to be the most efficient method of achieving the effect we wanted.

There are basically four or five types of terraced housing used on the layout so to avoid having to make too many patterns, as this is a very expensive process, we decided to concentrate on two types that, with slight modifications, could give us enough variations on the theme. You may think that there are numerous books and thousands of articles on the internet about terraced houses - most of us have lived in them and, indeed, some of us still do, but let me tell you it's not as easy as you think. One the first things we discovered was that most Victorian terraces turn out to be Edwardian! The builders at Leamington purchased areas of land and, just as they do today, built properties to suit three different markets: Cheap, or 'Affordable' to be politically correct, Middle Market and Luxury Villas. Although how you would

LEFT: This row of terraces was complicated to build. It is called Clapham Terrace and the actual buildings can still be seen at Leamington to this day. We built the terrace here on Christmas Day 2008.

describe a row of terraced houses as 'Luxury Villas' is beyond me – it just goes to show how little estate agent language has changed over the years!

The part of our layout that's nearest to the viewer is what is known as Old Leamington, although I venture that a more apt title would be 'Working Class Leamington'. These houses and the shops in the foreground of the model date back to pre-railway days and were far cheaper or 'affordable' than those built some time later to the north of the railway.

When we first had sight of the plans we were struck by how unusual they all were and we were eager to see more evidence of the actual buildings. We had decided to take a stand at the local Leamington Spa model show in January and we asked for photographs of the area and any input of local knowledge anyone might have. We hit

ABOVE: This photograph shows how buildings can be used to block a view. In this case the buildings are Handford Place, a row of workers' cottages. The perspex boxes that you can see mark the start of the town centre.

the jackpot in two areas! We found that one family's father had purchased all the Avenue Station drawings in the 1950s with a view to modelling it and they still had the plans! You can imagine our excitement to suddenly find ourselves in possession of a complete set of LNWR drawings for the Avenue Station. Our second stroke of luck was meeting a guy from the Town Architects' Office who not only was part of the planning team for Leamington Spa, but was also a keen modeller who was able to supply masses of really helpful information.

A chance comment from me started a fascinating piece of research. Although a Midlander, I live and work in London and I'm used to seeing houses with fire breaks ie where the partition wall is higher than the roof. Interestingly, this building feature became law after the Great Fire of London and I had always assumed that this applied only to buildings in the capital. I may be wrong, but I am sure I have never seen this feature on terraced houses in the Midlands yet here at Leamington all of the houses had this feature. I pointed this out to the architect, at the same time questioning why so many street names are actually places in London, for instance Clapham Terrace and Euston Place to name just two. A couple of weeks later he called me and confirmed that what I had suspected was true in that the majority of Leamington Spa had actually been built by builders from London.

RIGHT: Typical bay-fronted houses, showing how they fit the boxes.

I have to confess, my curiosity has been stirred and I'd love to get to the bottom of this but now is not the time so I'll stick to the facts as I know them at the moment. Houses in the Edwardian period conformed to some simple rules and, despite their fanciful description, these terraced houses in Handford Place were not built for luxury. Functionality, however, was key. Cheap houses would be built with dust floors and the first houses to be built on our layout were these very cheap houses. They were really comprised of two-up-and-two-down and one of the downstairs' rooms contained a range for cooking. The toilet would have been at the bottom of the garden or in the backyards.

BELOW: The pumphouse building shown as a kit of parts.

RIGHT: The pumphouse building as it is today.

These houses were pulled down in the mid 1950s to make way for the industrial estate which currently resides there but I can honestly say that it was these houses which really inspired me and gave me a passion to make the model in the first place.

The second and by far the biggest project was Clapham Terrace. Clapham Terrace is over 7ft long and is luxury accommodation compared to Handford Place. You can see that these houses have got bay windows which did not become a feature until after 1900 when the laws were relaxed on having protruding windows so things like porches and bay windows are very much an Edwardian feature. Whilst poorer people had the toilet outside, the residents of Clapham Terrace, being that little bit better off, had the toilet as part of the house and the kitchen became an addition.

One thing to point out if you are modelling this period, is that the modern flushing toilet, or water closet as it was known then, arguably invented by Thomas Crapper, did not become popular until around 1910/12. Prior to this, toilets had to be outside of the living accommodation because of the odour, so it's important to bear in mind that if the toilet is inside the house then it's probably a late addition or in a house which was built after the First World War. Although there is some debate about this, Thomas Crapper is reputed to have invented the revolutionary S bend which created a seal between the soil and the toilet seat. For our model, we created a kit to replicate the toilet.

All architectural modellers use a very simple, but brilliant, method of constructing buildings. They build them on Perspex boxes, thereby creating a solid base, which enables it to be moved in one piece but, more importantly, instantly glazes windows. I cannot recommend this method strongly enough as it's easy and saves you so much trouble.

We are now at the stage of working on what has turned out to be the biggest single job - the town centre. Again, all the simple rules that we talked about apply here such as using boxes and patterns but the difference, as I said earlier, is that the shops in Old Leamington are completely different from those on the other side of the bridge and the variety of types of shops became a real challenge for us to the point that we had to simplify this. As I've said before, the patterns to make these castings are expensive but if you want quality you need to pay for it and since there were a lot of shops on the layout then we considered the expense value for money.

The Avenue Station was built slightly differently. We made patterns for all the standard parts that the railway used, for the stations, windows, gutters, doors and facings, and we used foam board and Slater's Plasticard to cover the station. All the buildings are built in two stages – we build them, then paint them and then put them in situ. Details such as drain pipes and the like are added later.

You can see from pictures that we've not yet started on the General Station, because we are still trying to find the drawings, and we also need to start Brinklow Station.

BELOW: The completed pumphouse building sprayed grey. It is important to check the parts before adding to the perspex box.

RIGHT: Building up the shop.

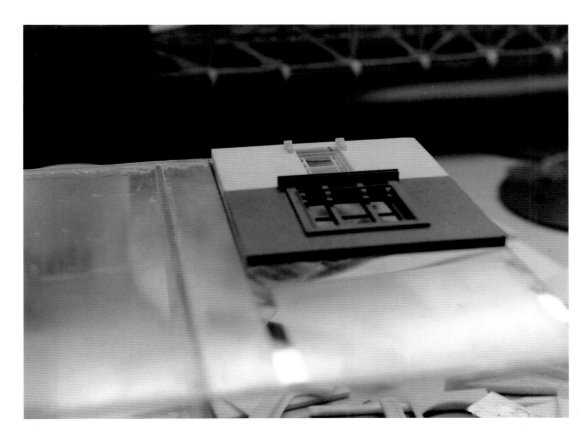

BELOW: The author rubbing down the parts before gluing.

LEFT: Clapham Terrace
before painting.

LEFT: The corner of
Clapham Terrace
and the canal.

RIGHT: Clapham terrace from further away.

BELOW: No 37193 passes on a fitted freight.

LEFT: The pumphouse building and the shop added to the perspex and placed in the street.

BELOW: This shows a view from Handford Place across to the town centre with the original pumphouse building in its place.

RIGHT: The main bridge in the town centre (in fact, two bridges). There are five different types of steel spans in the original structure. This was a huge task, built from plastic by Jason Bromley. Although the arches are completed there is still quite a lot of weathering and other finishing touches to be done.

BELOW: Looking towards the shed – this gives you some idea of the scale of what we are trying to achieve on the layout.

TRAIN FORMATIONS

Any decent railway enthusiast will tell you that, for them, one of the most interesting aspects of the railway is actually the train formations, whether they are passenger, parcels or goods. Therefore for us, a major part of the fun would be to recreate formations of trains of the period. Not just a string of coaches and carriages behind an engine, but something as close to typical as you could get. Leamington Spa is on what was the Great Western northern route and therefore had a special part to play in the make-up of trains.

The Great Western never really considered going to Birmingham or Wolverhampton as being important to it, with Bristol and the South West always representing its most important routes. The Northern Division tended to get quite old and clapped out stock which, although not good for the travelling public, was fantastic for the modeller as it was as late as 1957/58 before the BR Mk1 coaches became prominent.

Pre-1958 you would have been able to see almost any type of pre-nationalisation coaches, with lots of them still in their original liveries. On quite a few coaches, all that had been done was that the shield had been painted out or the roundel covered over and there are numerous photographs giving clear evidence of this. For me this was like strawberries for a donkey because the Great Western Northern Division coaches were a great passion of mine - particularly with the last 70-footers used on the Birkenheads.

With the probable exceptions of Highland or Great Eastern Railway stock, Leamington saw coaches from every region. I can remember seeing Gresleys in teak! What fantastic coaches - dirty they may have been, but teak and splendid they certainly were!

LEFT: The Class 40 shows its power on a coal train. The 40s can pull anything on the layout.

Right from the beginning of the project it was always my goal to try to recreate the early to mid-1950s because that's when I fell under the spell of railways. Consequently, this was the element of the modelling project that I personally looked forward to the most.

The thing I don't understand is just how so many people, who can get picky over the locomotives, don't have the same attention to detail when it comes to what they pull. Go to shows and you'll see what I mean because this is common to all gauges. You'd think that with a superb range of 4mm coaches to choose from, meticulousness would be the order of day because, presumably, all of us who model a railway have been on the real thing. It never ceases to amaze me, therefore, when I see so many layouts with no first class, no restaurants and no full brake coaches.

The thing I remember about my days on the platform at Leamington is that you were always surprised by what you saw. Things were never what I expected them to be. This was the Western Region, so I thought that Great Western coaches would have been used all the time. How wrong I was because the truth was that in fact there were frequently more LMS coaches in the rake than I would have ever anticipated and there were quite a few different designs in the same rake.

The colours almost all of the time were never the same, with some even still wearing pre-nationalisation colours. I very well remember the crimson and cream livery of nationalisation starting to spread across the network. Just as this was becoming pretty standard, the first of the new maroons appeared followed in 1957 by the

BELOW: A beautiful re-creation of how the railways used to be, highly detailed 70ft toplight coaches built by John Turton and painted by Alan Brackenborough.

prenationalisation colours. At no point in the 1950s or 1960s did I see just one livery as we did in the 1970s. With the wagon fleet in a right old state, the colours could be anything and there were still loads of former private owner wagons so there was plenty to see.

Like everything else on the layout, it was about choosing trains that would best represent the time as it would have been impossible to model any one day at Leamington Spa. By the mid 1970s there were still over 60 different variations of coaches and over 30 different types that you could have seen. If we look at Great Western alone, you could still see Dean, Churchward, Collett and Hawksworth coaches and there were still some second class coaches although they had been downgraded. There were smoking and non-smoking and, of course, ladies-only coaches.

We decided that we would have seven trains that would represent the Western Region - one Teak, two Southern rakes and six LMS containing period and steel stock. Train lengths depended on the time of year and could be strengthened if the demand had called for it but we chose to model summer when the trains were longer. Trains then were so unlike today and there were no, or very few, strict train sets but from studying photos of the era, you can average most trains out at about seven coaches. Yes, there were twelve-coach trains but there were also four-coach trains. Other than local trains, all trains would have carried a first-class-only coach and even a suburban train would have composites. All trains that went to London or came from London to Wolverhampton, or other such long distances, would always have carried a dining or buffet car. The Great Western cross-country sets had unique restaurant buffet cars and the named trains like the 'Royal Scott', the 'Cornishman' and the 'Intercity' all had full dining facilities and would have had a kitchen car. What a different world that was!

When you write it all down like this it sounds fascinating and you can easily forget the complexities involved but for our model layout we had to build well over 100 coaches. Not only did we have to make each coach, but we had to make the kits to make the coach! Take the bow enders, for example, as these were the most numerous coaches on the Western Region throughout the 1950s and 1960s. There were full brakes, brake thirds, brake composites, all thirds, composites, all first, restaurant and nondescript saloons. That's 16 different sides and interiors and if you take a look at the Gresleys they had five different seat types! You can therefore grasp just how massive the task was and now, five years down the line, the wish list is even longer! Experience has taught me one thing, however, and that is there is a massive difference between

building one piece of rolling stock for the show case or exhibition and building it over 100 times - you tend to lose the will to live with the latter! The other problem is shorts. The more bits you put round the wheels, the more shorts you get. This is an area where compromise, rather than accuracy, is the order of the day and this is absolutely the right thing to do.

The 1950s were what could be called 'Old Britain' as it really was a hangover from the 1930s caused by the intervening war years. Not only was there a huge backlog of repairs to the wagon fleet, but, more importantly, there was a need to modernise what, even by the 1930s standards, had become an obsolete fleet. For instance, the mine owners never saw it as their priority or responsibility to maintain or improve their own wagons and in fact used the railways sidings to store them. This scenario is a microcosm of the history of railways, with private owners wanting the railway to pay their costs.

By the 1950s, the last of the wooden wagons should have been scrapped but the lack of money and the lack of materials meant that they carried on into the 1960s. For the benefit of the younger readers, in those days all long-distance freight mainly went by rail because there were no motorways, and coal was the biggest commodity moved by rail. Virtually every home in Britain still used coal for heating and every factory needed coal, as did all the power stations, which were coal powered. With this volume

ABOVE: We take wagons as seriously as locomotives. We spent months on the research for the presflos before we started to build them. There will be 14 in the train – ten yellow and four fawn.

of demand, you can see just how much coal there was to move and why the trains ran round the clock, 24 hours a day and seven days a week. There were yards all over Great Britain full of empty and full coal wagons.

Standing spotting at Leamington you would have seen coal trains trundling past all day at their 20mph and what you have to remember is that for every full train of coal there was a corresponding empty one going in the opposite direction so I felt this was an important part of the railway for us to model. What we wanted to try to do was to give an impression of the diversity of the wagons used and decided to recreate an up and down Great Western coal train and an LMR coal train but we realised that, because of the problems encountered with the way that MEK attacked the plastic body of the wagons, it would be very difficult to get empty wagons to look realistic. As luck would have it, I had been given a range of wagons of superb quality to produce as one-piece bodies and one of these was the standard Charles Roberts coal wagon. This model was absolutely the best I have ever seen in that it represented a coal wagon after use. In other words, everything had moved on the body because of the weight of the coal - if you look at used ones they bow outwards because of the density and weight of the coal they have carried. The problem with plastic moulds is that the opposite happens, they bow inwards because of the tension of MEK so you have to use card to keep them square, which is impractical if they

have an empty load. We decided to have one set of steel wagons that were becoming very common after the war, one train of wooden empties that would include all three different types of wooden wagon, some very big private owner ones and a fairly modern one with the large hoppers. This would allow us to play with our Class 25 diesels.

ABOVE: *City of Chester*, built by Dave Baker, painted by Alan Brackenborough, heads towards Birmingham during the West Coast closures.

The other type of wagon that was prevalent in the 1950s was the van. There were literally thousands of them and again trains ran all day with just vans so this was another feature that was important to us. Last but not least, were the pick-up trains. Photographers took more pictures of pick-up goods than they did of anything else because they were pretty and, dare we say it, easy to photograph! The train would go through local stations picking up and dropping off wagons and quite often would have no more than five or six wagons and a guard's van. These trains, funnily enough, were a problem for us! The big trains are easy! Small trains like pick-up freights clog up our storage system, but we have to have them.

Most of the wagons have been built by two or three people. Colin Foster has built the majority, with Michelle Davidson taking credit for quite a few, and then there was me! I decided to take on the train of empties. Now, just in case you are sitting there thinking, 'no big deal building a wagon', you'd be absolutely right but just to put it into context, when you've got to build 65 at a time, the word 'easy' isn't what springs to mind! As I have said many times in this book, every aspect of this project was an enormous task and this again is evidenced when you consider that our three coal trains made up over 150 wagons. If you work out that each wagon, unpainted, takes over an hour to build, that's an awful lot of work! This task would be impossible without Parkside Dundas Kits, Slaters and our own as it would be an absolute impossibility to build all these trains with etched kits.

BELOW: Nos 10000 and 10001 on the diverted 'Royal Scot'. The engines were built and painted by Simon Atkinson.

LEFT: No 4904 '*Binnegar Hall*', built by Paul Hannah and painted by Conrad Cooper, heads a mixed freight towards Leamington.

LEFT: No D6822 with a Presflo cement wagon in tow.

RIGHT: An interloper! An Eastern Region train on its way back to Newcastle with a Special. As many people know, I do the teaking myself. If I didn't enjoy it there probably wouldn't be as much of it on the layout. For me it's a fond reminder of watching the railway in days gone by when I was just a kid.

RIGHT: Somewhat bedraggled and bemused! A '57xx' and an '8750' trundling with a permanent way train.

Seagull with a full rake of Pullman coaches on an excursion - it just proves you can make an excuse for doing just about everything on the layout.

RIGHT: No. 5553, one of the WHR Trust engines, with the Leamington Stratford auto train. These lasted until 1960 and show the first vehicle still in wartime brown with the toplights painted over. I believe Didcot is the only preserved railway that has ever used this livery yet in the 1950s there were so many vehicles to be seen in it on the railway.

RIGHT: No 7819 *Hinton Manor* on a very typical GW/BR train, a three-coach bow-ended rake. There was more bow-ended stock during the early to mid-1950s on the Western Region than anything else. However, they are very tricky vehicles to model and rarely modelled today.

BUILDING THE ENGINES

My first model book, *A Train for Life*, was a tribute really to the builders mainly of the 10mm locos which were not built specifically for Leamington and therefore the following names who were the builders of the locomotives for Leamington may be new to you. The main steam locomotive builders were Dave Baker and Paul Hannah, with some very nice additions from Peter Roles. Simon Atkinson, John Turton and Roger Manton were mainly responsible for the diesels.

Everybody always approaches locomotives with stars in their eyes - and, let's be honest, so did we! In fact, it was only the time it takes to build a locomotive which kept us in check, otherwise we would have let our imaginations run riot and we would have got carried away.

When we began the project, the idea was to have a typical day at Leamington Spa and the locos and the stock would be made to give the best impression of this. We quickly realised, however, that because Leamington had two stations (which of course included the LMS) the variety of locomotives was going to be that much greater. Originally, we all agreed that we weren't going to get too precious if somebody wanted to run their favourite locomotive but then we realised that we had to be a little bit cautious.

Another pre-conceived idea was that we would probably have the odd 'Peak' or Class 40 diesel – well, that's what we thought! The reality, of course, was that our enthusiasm got the better of us to the point that we are now even building trains so that we can run the later Rail Blue period. Where possible, we use Alan Harris wheels but Slaters are kind enough to always do us new wheels when we need them.

LEFT: No 7026 *Tenby Castle* sits on Hatton Bank.

The painting of all our locomotives is carried out by either Alan Brackenborough or Conrad Cooper and we are delighted that we have been fortunate enough to have the services of these master craftsmen. I have seen so many really superb models spoilt by poor painting and that must be soul destroying for the builder. I accept that getting an expert to do the painting for you may be expensive, but I consider it money well spent to leave this task to those who have this incredible skill.

At this point, I would like to mention a book I bought recently by Ian Rathbone called *A Modellers Handbook of Painting and Lining* which is a fantastic and intuitive read. Ian makes it sound all so easy that he makes you want to reach for the bow pen! Fabulous book, Ian, but I'm pleased I had the sense to resist putting it into practice when we had the experts to do it!

BELOW: The last 'Star' in the Midlands, *Glastonbury Abbey*, is light engine at Hatton.

ABOVE: No 1016 *County of Hants*, one of the Wolverhampton 'Counties' on Hatton. Built by Paul Hannah and painted by Conrad Cooper.

RIGHT: No 5088 *Llanthony Abbey* was also built by Paul Hannah and painted by Conrad Cooper. This was another Wolverhampton engine.

LEFT: We used to see lots of Southern engines at Leamington, particularly on football specials. No 35023 *Holland Africa Line*, painted by Alan Brackenborough, is on its way to Birmingham.

BELOW: The locomotive from the fireman's side.

RIGHT: There's always space on the layout for the 'Britannias'. Leamington saw 'Britannias' all the time on the West Coast and No 70046 *Anzac* was a regular visitor.

BELOW: *Anzac* from the fireman's side.

The '38' pulls the big mineral train.

BUILDING THE STOCK

It took only one session to which members brought their own stock for us to realise that it was never going to be a practical idea for us to run our own stock. The damage sustained was unbelievable and made us realise that on a project this size it would be impossible for the stock to be moved about so that all the stock would have to belong with the layout. This meant that we would only accept visiting locomotives.

It's only when you have a running day that you realise the full capacity of the layout and then the whole project takes on a different dimension. It doesn't sound much when you say that you have 14 storage sidings, which means that you run 14 trains. However, if you are running say between 6- and 11-coach trains, that's up to 60 coaches! If you're

RIGHT: Bank Holiday weekend was spent adding wheels to the wagons.

running four or five freights of over 45 wagons, that's around 200 wagons - and that's not counting the odd wagon scattered around the layout to make it look realistic!

At this point I would remind you that we were building the layout ourselves with very little outside help and it was never in our plans to build wagons or coaches so we sub-contracted them out. The wagons were built mainly by two builders, Colin Foster and Michelle Davidson. All of the mineral wagons and most of the box vans were built by Colin and most of the specialist vehicles by Michelle. We are probably only one third of the way through the vans that we need and we have just taken delivery of the big hopper coal train. I think this has proved a bigger task than Colin had expected, not to mention how mentally challenging building 45 of any wagon must be - but then, of course, on a layout this size, it's simply never about building one of anything!

We have found that the biggest problem we have is wagon wheels (and I'm not talking about the chocolate variety!). The task of cleaning the wheels on a regular basis has proved impracticable because the last time that we tried it it took us seven hours just to clean the mineral train and then we began to lose the will to live! We continue to search for the perfect solution but we haven't found it yet and all suggestions would be gratefully received.

ABOVE: I love the blood and custard coach livery because of the way that it weathered. You can see on this rake of bow-ended stock how we pick out the doors and window surrounds. This is done with a thick dilution of black in turps which allows the dirt to shoot down the door joints. After this dries, we use chalk brushed on slowly and built up over several different sessions. This set was worked on by Paul Marshall Potter and the author.

ABOVE: CCT built by Roger Manton on the back of his Class 25, another local paper train with 'return to Wolverhampton Low Level' scribbled on it.

Weathering was also an enormous task and - as explained in the 'Weathering' chapter - we used a 'broad brush' approach.

We get a certain sense of enjoyment by running prototypical lengths. This means that we have to lift the train one wagon at a time and have the enjoyment of seeing the buffers going up and down gradients. Recently we had a visitor who brought a very nice looking 'Black 5' and was staggered when he opened the controller to see the wheels just slip and when he actually pulled the wagon by hand he was shocked at the weight. But this is not surprising, really, when you think of it, as 45 wagons, even plastic wagons, with white metal fittings are always going to be heavy.

Our plans for the future include our beloved cement train, an oil train and a breakdown train. Although having said that, without a doubt somebody will come along and show us a wagon that we like and that will completely change our strategy.

LEFT: This shows a rake of very distressed wagons built by Pete Thompson and will form part of a new concept that we are working on.

BELOW: BR Mark 1 blue and grey coaches on commonwealth bogies, made and painted by Roger Manton. The window chalk says 'return to Leamington'.

RIGHT: Roger Manton's Class 25 on a newspaper train heads for Birmingham.

BELOW: More of the author's handiwork. We are not afraid to do something out of the ordinary and spent a lot of time experimenting. Note the hole in the wagon.

WEATHERING

Now, this part of our decision-making strategy was easy - ALL of our stock had to be weathered!

Just to correct a common misconception, for anyone who thinks that the weathering process is simply making the model dirty, you couldn't be further from the reality! This is an art - and I mean an art - and it requires careful scrutiny of the way that dirt accumulates on the railway. Again, I can't over emphasise the importance of research and examination, so first let's get answers to two questions: what colour is dirt and where does it come from?

When it comes to getting dirty you'll find that locomotives are different to coaches, which are different to wagons, which are different to buildings! So let's start with the locomotives. If you think about what happens when they bring the real thing out of the paint shop, the first thing they do is to cover it in coal dust and spray it with water as they fill the tender. Just for good measure, they'll splash it with oil to lubricate it and then whack a dirty great fire into the firebox which heats the whole thing up! As the smoke starts to belch all over it, they have already created the effect of one large dirty locomotive without even moving a wheel! Once it's stuck into gear and the regulator is opened you will get a different sort of dust emanating from the track and platforms, and not forgetting the dust that's in the atmosphere as well. Exposed to all of this, in just 24 hours you will be looking at a very weathered locomotive.

If you look at good colour pictures from the 1950s, you will see that a pattern emerges on green engines which is perversely caused by the cleaning process.

LEFT: Roger Manton's 08 shunter sits ticking over in Brinkwell Yard, while a fitted van train passes.

I'm specifically talking about the very dark sheen which gathers in the corners and particularly on the top of the cladding of green engines. This effect is entirely due to the practice of using paraffin to clean the locomotive which, as it heats up, causes this reaction on the paintwork.

Having discussed locomotives we now come to coaches. Coaches obviously weather in a completely different way. Whereas the locomotive has heat and oil, these two elements are, by and large, missing on coaches but are replaced by dust from the track and the dust from the ash which is obviously emitted from the locomotive's chimney. In that emission, there is both water and oil which is dispersed all over the coaches. Picture this: it's a bright, sunny day and the coaches are going from Birmingham to Paddington, powered along by a 'King' which for over 2½ hours has been steaming and covering them with its related muck. It's doing 100 miles at, let's say, 45mph through various industrial and rural landscapes. Remember we're in England so, typically, on the return journey at some point the sun goes in and it starts to rain on all the dust that's collected on the coaches from the outward journey. Because it's travelling in a forward direction, the rain isn't washing the dust down in a vertical flow but rather the residue is now travelling along the coaches and indeed gathering in all the corners of all the door frames, all the louvres and all the windows. The Great British Climate kicks in

ABOVE: No 1055 *Western Advocate* powers through Brinklow. I'm not sure whether a 'Western' ever went this route but it did when Roger said so!

yet again, say, at Banbury, and the rain stops, to be replaced by a sun that will dry all the deposits on the coaches and again they are at the mercy of what the locomotive spews out! All of this could happen four times a day, six days a week before the cleaning job is undertaken.

Before we move on, there is another contributory factor that bears mention and that is the position of the coaches on the journeys. Outward, the front carriage gets contaminated the most and the last one the least because, of course, the further away from the engine the less dirt is imparted. However, on the return journey, the reverse will be the case - as the bible says, 'the last shall be first and the first shall be last'! If a coach does four journeys a day then it will be evenly coated with an awful lot of grime and you can imagine the intensity of it.

Ah yes, I hear you say, but they get washed! And you'd be right, but this in itself caused another problem. From as early as the 1920s, the railways used a cutting agent in its water - a soda-type substance to loosen the dirt, thereby making it easier to clean. However, not only did it loosen the dirt, it also had the same stripping effect on the varnish and, once that had deteriorated, on the colours. This can be no more evident than in the blood and custard livery of the 1950s which particularly suffered from wear and tear. Just as a personal note here, I love the way that the blood and custard weathered and I loved to see all the different ways that they faded. The pigment in

BELOW: Another view of Roger Manton's *Western Advocate.*

these particular paints was not that strong so on one rake you the colours would
have deteriorated from yellow cream to white cream and from deep blood to
anaemia!

The carriage washing plants became a feature of the 1970s and certain ones had an
effect on the way they cleaned their trains, the most infamous being Laira shed on the
Western Region. The Laira carriage wash was the best BR paint stripper that they
ever used, but for modellers it's a godsend!

Having covered locomotives and coaches, we now come to a really difficult area -
wagons. Wagons were the poor relations of all the rolling stock and they suffered
every abuse known to wagonkind! Because they were functional and carried goods,
they were not really cared for provided their wheels kept turning. When it comes to
modelling, however, the wagons have their own moments of glory because this is one

ABOVE: A rake of BR
Mk 1 suburban
coaches. The faded
colours and
weathering are
faithfully reproduced.

ABOVE: We can never have too many vans. As with the railway in the 1950s, there were more vans than virtually anything else – only coal wagons out numbered them.

of the areas where, as a modeller, you can have fantastic fun and I've seen some stunning weathering on wagons - and I mean stunning! Fabulous representations of rust, weathering, replaced parts, broken plants, chipped roofs, cracked planking - you name it, I've seen it on some unbelievable models.

It was, however, in this area when we were building Leamington Spa that we had to keep our imagination and passion in check. We had to constantly remind each other - well, to be truthful, Mike had to keep reminding us - that we were modelling from 50ft and therefore we were looking for an overall impression. As enjoyable as it would have been, it would have been impractical to try and achieve this high standard of wagon weathering. Were we to have pursued our natural inclination on weathering wagons then, to give you some idea of the time it would have taken, if everyone reading this book was to do just one wagon, we'd be getting the angels to help us finish it! So when it came to wagons, we had to be very strict about the level of detail because putting one sensational wagon in the middle of the layout would have made all the others look silly.

And finally, just when you thought it was all over, we have to look at the buildings! Buildings need weathering too and, just as for coaches, the same rules apply. The only difference is that they don't move! Our experience has shown that the best approach to weathering buildings is to do it over a long period of time so this is another of our long-running jobs, but we know that we will get there.

LEFT: They don't all have to be big engines! Roger's No 08693 sits between shunting duties.

BELOW: *Glastonbury Abbey* shows off a clean but weathered BR engine. The weathering was done by Fred Lewis and this is how I remember the engines looking - even when cleaned they always had a black tinge at the top

ABOVE: Brian Daniel's visiting No 4979 *Wootton Hall*. This again shows Brian's version of BR dirt.

RIGHT: No 37193, Brian's Class 37, with working headlights and fabulous weathering.

RUNNING THE LAYOUT

As the layout has started to come together, more time has been given over to running it, but in the not-too-distant future we will have to adopt a slightly different approach. At the moment, we are still using it more or less as a test track but in the next year, when there are more train formations, then we will introduce a timetable which should be a lot more fun.

I think we all get a lot of fun from seeing a locomotive that someone has built overcome the rigours of Leamington because, I kid you not, this layout is a killer on locomotives. You cannot just open the controller and leave it: you need to drive the locomotive and you have to learn where the inclines are because there's a couple which always catch new operators out. The fun bit is learning how to pick your locomotive up once you start to slip! It's very easy to spot on Leamington those operators that are used to the hill or the gradients coming out of the fiddle siding. You can also tell by the way that they avoid certain trains with certain engines. All of my engines weigh between 2¾ kg and 3½ kg which is the weight needed to lift some of these trains and keep them moving.

We also have to pay a lot of attention to keeping all the parts oiled on an engine. If we leave a locomotive for two or three weeks and allow it to dry out, then the consequences for running it without oil will not make the owner happy! The constant problem that we have with a layout of this size is the problem of dirty wheels. And we don't yet know completely our way around it, despite our efforts. We've tried all the cleaning systems that everyone says work but can find no substitute for cleaning the track with white spirit and

LEFT: This shows the problem of building in scale at this magnitude. There's no way that if something comes off in the middle of the layout we can get to it as it is 20ft across at its widest section. Although there is still lots of work to do, the signals do give you a fair idea of all the movement that took place in Leamington.

ABOVE: Obviously all main line stations have lots of sidings. This shows the banks and the ends of the sidings. Because of the width, this has been narrowed down considerably on the layout.

using a light stone or cleaning the loco wheels with MEC and buffing with a fibre pencil. If you tell me a method of cleaning over 4,000 wheels on the coaches and wagons and I'll tell you it can't be done! Having tried and failed to come up with any workable system we find ourselves understanding the frustration felt about painting the Forth Bridge! No matter how hard we try to pre plan, something always goes wrong!

With the benefit of hindsight, the layout is far too wide and, with the sidings in the station, far too ambitious. The best layouts are probably, at their widest, as far as an arm can reach. Sidings in awkward places, albeit prototypical, don't work on model railways because they become dust traps and are unsightly. Again, with the 20:20 vision of hindsight, I wish we had taken more time on the sanding and ballasting because it is so important for running.

When we set out to build Leamington Spa our dream was to try to achieve an overall impression of the station for the viewer and to take O gauge to where it had never been before. We were determined to avoid getting bogged down with arguments and I'm delighted to be able to say that we're all still enjoying the trip. Although we have lost a couple of friends along the way, our thoughts are with them and their pictures hang in our 'Modeller's Gallery'. We remember their contribution with great thanks and fondness. Some of the members are now 'in the winter of their lives' but despite advancing years, I wonder how the hell they still achieve such levels of enthusiasm as they do!

It's not my railway. It belongs to all the guys that have worked on it and we have enjoyed some of the funniest banter I've ever had the privilege to be part of. Throughout the year (and normally on Sunday mornings) we have regular club visits from all over the UK. We are only sorry that it can't be more but at the moment is still takes at least 12 of us to operate and most of the guys only get a pass-out on a Sunday — a pass-out on a Saturday as well would be a bit too much to ask of their wives and partners although I have to give credit to these ladies who offer us tremendous support.

Despite any critical comments in the book, Leamington is fantastic. We have had a lot of fun and it's not finished yet — there's still a long way to go! Would we choose to break all the barriers down in the way that we have had to, if we had to do it all over again? Well, maybe, just maybe, we would!

As I reach the end of this book, which I hope you enjoy, I find myself thinking in my music world and the lyrics of John Lennon spring to mind: 'You may think I'm a dreamer, but I'm not the only one, I hope one day you'll join us . . .' and decide to take on the challenge of moving this fantastic hobby of ours forward.

RIGHT: Notice the bike outside the signalbox. This was built by the author from an etch kit - I won't be building another one!

LEFT: 'WD 'Austerity'. These were regular visitors and it seems strange now to think that we hankered after the '2-8-0s' after they'd gone. It just proves the old adage 'you never know what you've got until it's gone'.

LEFT: This shows Napton Canal. Although, far from finished, it gives you an impression of how it will look. On the real Leamington it's straight, but for us it needed to have a dog leg. The flowers might be a touch too bright but this will be rectified.

ABOVE: You can just see the cycleway in the foreground. This is a fantastic spot to from which to view the trains running.

RIGHT: The canal bridges. These are standard Great Western style and in the background are the LNW girder bridges which carry the GW main line. The points at the back are the entrance to the shed.

A peek over the hill. This is Mike's imaginary train-spotting viewing point and it shows off well Mike's cycleway and dead tree. Also, note how much lighting it takes.

DCC

Five years ago, when we started the layout, DCC (digital command control) was far more complicated and frightening than it needed to be. From the beginning, there was never really an option for us because only DCC gave us the freedom that we needed so the layout is run on DCC. There have been copious reports written about this system and in my opinion some of these are quite misleading so, in an attempt to redress the balance, I thought I would pass on my first-hand experience with DCC having used it for four years.

Without a doubt, once you've used DCC I guarantee you will never want to use any other system. Forget what's gone before — clockwork (thankfully) rests in peace! — and embrace this giant leap in technology. 'Embrace' is the optimum word here because if you try to understand the intrinsic technical detail of the system then you will be on a hiding to nothing. My advice is to leave that understanding to those people who want to create the systems. Your job is to run the model and if you simply follow the rules of which wire fits where and how to address the chip then you will find that your layout is far more interesting and much more user friendly.

The DCC system is extensive. Indeed, I'd go so far as to say that it is capable of offering more applications than 99.9% of modellers will ever use. Resist being blinded by the science of it because the truth is that even though a Digital Command Centre might boast that it is capable of running 9,999 locos at any one time, this impressive credential is irrelevant to most modellers.

LEFT: Another one of Dave's lovely LNER engines - this time a 'V2', *The Sapper.*

Let's get down to the fact that it's only a train controller, if that's what you want it to be, and the really interesting element of this component is that it operates more than one train at any one time on the same track. It's as simple as entering the coach for the locomotive. All locos have numbers - because that's the point of train spotting - and you really don't need to know much more than that, because once you've learned to programme the locomotive, everything else is simple. I suggest that we leave the electronic boffins to get on with their bit, and that the rest of us simply move trains.

From the beginning we've used the loco numbers as the addresses and we use the Zimo DCC System which is expensive but it is money well spent because it is in a class of its own. Obviously, before you commit to the expense you have to know that what you are buying will suit your requirements and this prompts me to issue a warning about the cost of DCC. I once represented Zimo for the UK and most of the enquiries I received were from 4mm modellers who would open the conversation with the classic line 'I've got 76 locos to chip'. At that point I might as well have put the phone down because I have yet to see any layouts or collections that could run this amount. On further questioning it was obvious that the customer was a collector not a modeller so my warning to you is that it is important to remember that DCC is for people who run trains not for those who collect them. Chips cost from between £15 to £40.

Now we enter the Twilight Zone where you can take this one stage further because the system allows you to add both sound and lights! As I said earlier, the capabilities of DCC are endless - the question for you now is how deep are your pockets! The system can do anything you require it to just as long as you can afford it.

On our layout, we have the advantage of space because we are modeling in 7mm scale so we therefore found it easy to fit speakers into our diesels. Without wishing to sound too controversial, we have chosen to avoid the steam sound as we haven't heard a system yet where the speakers will carry the steam loco frequencies.

Once you understand the way the wiring works this is also a lot simpler and a lot tidier. We can switch off the DCC from one circuit so visiting locos can run but then this isolates storage sidings which inhibits us crossing with DCC.

In many aspects of the layout, compromise has been key to its success and that is never truer than it is here. Sound has to be a compromise. We can all get carried away with the right sound for the right engine, and that's fine when it comes to diesels but it's completely different when applied to steam. With the diesel it's relatively simple but

RIGHT: How did this engine get in here again! It must be on the way back! These were very unusual looking engines but I can say No 62723 *Nottinghamshire* runs beautifully, as do all Steph Torres engines.

RIGHT: One of my favourite locomotives, No 6022 *King Edward III*. Built by Paul Hannah, painted by Conrad Cooper, it was a replacement for the one I sold in a rare moment of madness!

nonetheless it is absolutely fundamental where the microphone is placed when you are recording the sound because, once you've fitted the sound, you can't go back.

Having installed the sound to your satisfaction you then might be thinking: 'Well, do I place a light unit in now?' If you do that, though, do add a smoke unit to your steam locomotive but then that poses a slightly different question because, although you now have sound in the locomotive, you have no sound in the wagons or coaches, and if you are going to be so pedantic about sound in the locomotive, should you not extrapolate this to wagons and coaches? A line must be drawn and that line is called compromise. In building the layout our compromise, as far as sound was concerned, was to limit it to the locomotive.

You can get similarly carried away with lights. The locomotive has lights so why not light signals or lights on coaches? On a layout this size it was not possible to go down this route and again we compromised and agreed that sound was in, lights were out - no pun intended!

Our ultimate aim is to control the whole layout from a computer including all the signals and points but that is both a job and a book for the future.

BELOW: Another one of Dave Baker's locomotives, this time No 69523, an 'N2' tank. Painted and lined by Alan Brackenborough, this really is a gorgeously pretty engine.

RIGHT: 'King Arthur' No 30740 *Merlin*, built by Peter Roles and painted by Alan Brackenborough. This was part of the late John Porter's collection.

BELOW: *Merlin* from the other side.

LEFT: A BR Standard 5 with a Southern van. The engine runs as good as it looks and was built by Dave Baker using our own chassis and a DJB body.

BELOW: The 'Crabs' were certainly distinctive locomotives. We are lucky that we preserved one. This engine belongs to Arthur Magee.

RIGHT: Dave Baker's 'B1' No 61201 looks as beautiful as it runs. It was built by Dave Baker and painted by Alan Brackenborough.

BELOW: No 45600 *Bermuda*, built by Dave Baker and painted by Alan Brackenborough. One of the 'Jubilees' on the layout that pull everything

PHOTOGRAPHING THE LAYOUT

One of the pleasures of Leamington Spa is being able to invite professional photographers to capture the detail and life of the layout particularly when running trains. The size of the layout means it is difficult to capture the scale of our work in progress but the book concludes with some inspirational shots of a variety of locations and models around the layout, many in live steam, from photographer Chris Nevard of *Hornby Magazine* and *Model Rail* magazine.

We set out to make a model of a railway. The following photographs show what we've achieved but there is a long way to go. A few of us that started the project never saw it this far. So these Chris Nevard photos are in memory of them. We miss them very much.

Tempus fugit!

LEFT: Close up of D222 *Laconia*.

ABOVE: **No 2887 and the blue 'King' pass at Hatton Bank**

LEFT AND OPPOSITE: **No 1028 at Hatton Bank.**

THIS PAGE: No 7819 passes the signal box.

OVERLEAF: No 2887 heads of through the countryside.

FINAL PAGE: The blue 'King' finale.